APPALACHIAN TRAIL
On My Mind

The Globe Pequot Press

GUILFORD, CONNECTICUT

Shenandoah National Park, Virginia TERRY DONNELLY

Title page photo: Alan Briere
Map by Stefanie Ward, © The Globe Pequot Press

Library of Congress Cataloging-in-Publication Data is available.
ISBN 0-7627-2525-7

Manufactured in the United States of America
First Edition/First Printing

CANADA

MAINE

Mt. Katahdin

VERMONT

NEW HAMPSHIRE

Lake Huron

Lake Ontario

NEW YORK

MASSACHUSETTS

CONNECTICUT

RHODE ISLAND

MICHIGAN

Lake Erie

PENNSYLVANIA

NEW JERSEY

OHIO

DELAWARE

MARYLAND

INDIANA

WEST VIRGINIA

Atlantic

VIRGINIA

KENTUCKY

Ocean

NORTH CAROLINA

TENNESSEE

Springer Mtn.

SOUTH CAROLINA

ALABAMA

GEORGIA

Appalachian Trail ▪▪▪▪▪▪▪▪

Sunset over Brasstown Bald, Chattahoochee National Forest, Georgia TOM TILL

Morning mist in the Chattahoochee National Forest, Georgia BART SMITH

Our first day showed us what we could expect in Georgia. Persephone and Spring had not yet risen from the underworld. With icy invitation, the wind gusted through the barren maples and oaks. Dead vines were rolled like barbed wire at the foot of skeletal trees.

—STEVE SHERMAN & JULIA OLDER,
Georgia—78 Miles

Trees bloom with the promise of spring at Amicalola Falls State Park, Georgia. TOM TILL

The first hint of spring has come to the hollows of north Georgia's hills . . . like a Seurat painting, a dotting of yellow-green leaf tips, red buds and white dogwood bracts over-laying dry winter hillsides of sinuous tree trunks and gray-brown leaves.

—ROBERT ALDEN RUBIN,
On the Beaten Path: An Appalachian Pilgrimage

TOM TILL

Enjoying the glory of spring on the Appalachian Trail,
Dicks Creek Gap, Georgia BART SMITH / CREST PHOTOGRAPHY

A rainbow hovers in the mist of Taccoa Falls, Georgia. JAMES RANDKLEV / LARRY ULRICH STOCK

A spider explores a lady's slipper on the trail. TOM TILL

A road, a mile of kingdom, I am king
Of banks and stones and every blooming thing.

—PATRICK KAVANAGH, "Inniskeen Road: July Evening"

Dawn's gray light rises over Cheoah Bald, Nantahala National Forest, North Carolina.

Wind swirled fog through the trees and across our path. . . . Sky and mountain disappeared; trees and fog remained. . . . No rapturous "see the world" view; there was no world . . . only darkened tree trunks, tangled branches, wispy fog. Strange, striking. Perhaps even . . . beautiful.

—MIC LOWTHER, *Walking North*

Large flowered trillium and fringed phacelia cover a hillside in Great Smoky Mountains National Park. TERRY DONNELLY

The bright pink flower of a dwarf rhododendron peeks out of a rocky slope, Tennessee. BART SMITH / CREST PHOTOGRAPHY

Sunrise over the Smoky Mountains, Great Smoky Mountains National Park

Daybreak casts a rosy glow over Fontana Lake, Great Smoky Mountains National Park. BART SMITH

Horses graze in the early morning fog at Cades Cove, Tennessee.

Flowering dogwoods herald the arrival of spring, Tennessee.

The Appalachian Trail is spiced with names as distinctive and homespun as Sassafras Gap, Panther Creek, Roaring Fork, Buzzards Rock, Dogtail Corners, Cranberry Pond, Music Mountain, Shady Valley, Buttermilk Falls, Devils Den, Breezy Point, and Podunk Brook.

—ANN & MYRON SUTTON, *A Special Dignity in Naming*

The morning sun dapples branches and field, Tennessee. MARY LIZ AUSTIN

To walk. To see. To see what you see.

—BENTON MACKAYE

The surface of the Little River reflects its lush surroundings, Tennessee. TERRY DONNELLY

An oak branch in autumn, Tennessee TERRY DONNELLY

A hint of autumn colors the canopy of the Smoky
Mountains, North Carolina. MARY LIZ AUSTIN

An evening view from Lovers Leap, Cherokee National Forest, North Carolina BART SMITH / CREST PHOTOGRAPHY

The moon spreads its wintry light over "Beauty Spot," Pisgah National Forest, North Carolina. BART SMITH

A drowsy, dreamy influence seems to hang over the land. . . . The whole neighborhood abounds with local tales, haunted spirits, and twilight superstitions.

—WASHINGTON IRVING,
The Legend of Sleepy Hollow

Wildflowers bloom along the trail to Sinking Creek Valley, Virginia. BART SMITH / CREST PHOTOGRAPHY

Afoot and light hearted I take to the open road,
Healthy, free, the world before me,
The long brown path before me, leading wherever I choose.

—WALT WHITMAN, "Song of the Open Road"

Hikers stop to enjoy the sights in the Mount Rogers National Recreation Area, Virginia.
LAURENCE PARENT

A wild pony at rest, Grayson Highlands, Virginia
BART SMITH

March sunrise over Shenandoah National Park, Virginia BART SMITH / CREST PHOTOGRAPHY

The Shenandoah River Valley in all of its springtime glory TERRY DONNELLY

Flame azalea adds a bright splash of orange to its green environs, Virginia.

*Countless hikers take to the AT in springtime with one goal
in mind: to see the spectacular flame azalea in bloom.*

—DAVID EMBLIDGE, editor, *The Appalachian Trail Reader*

Sunset paints a palette of colors over the Blue Ridge Mountains, Virginia.

Summit rocks on Hawksbill Mountain, Virginia TOM TILL

Spring fog shrouds lichen-covered oaks, Shenandoah National Park, Virginia. TERRY DONNELLY

Cluster of false hellebore TERRY DONNELLY

Something hidden. Go and find it. Go and look behind
the Ranges—Something lost . . . and waiting for you.

—RUDYARD KIPLING

Harpers Ferry National Historical Park, West Virginia TOM TILL

Scenes from Harpers Ferry, a historic town on the Shenandoah and Potomac Rivers
THIS PAGE, TOM TILL; *OPPOSITE*, BART SMITH / CREST PHOTOGRAPHY

Morning over the Potomac, Maryland BART SMITH

A particularly rocky section of trail near Wind Gap, Pennsylvania BART SMITH

Redbud bursts forth along Trough Creek, Pennsylvania. LARRY ULRICH

Nearly everyone I talked to had some gruesome story involving a guileless acquaintance who had gone off hiking the trail with new boots and come stumbling back two days later with a bobcat attached to his head or dripping blood from an armless sleeve and whispering in a hoarse voice, "Bear!" before lapsing into unconsciousness.

—BILL BRYSON, *A Walk in the Woods*

A patchwork piece of Pennsylvania farm country BART SMITH

The Boulder Field at Hickory Run State Park,
Pennsylvania LARRY ULRICH

A goldfinch perches on a flower at the Wallkill National Wildlife Preserve, New Jersey. BART SMITH

Oh, fare thee well, I must be gone,
And leave you for a while,
Wherever I go I will return,
If I go ten thousand miles.

—TRADITIONAL ENGLISH BALLAD

High water, the result of a storm, can be seen from Kittatinny Mountain; Delaware Water Gap, New Jersey and Pennsylvania. TOM TILL

Buttermilk Falls (Pennsylvania), Delaware Water Gap National Recreation Area, New Jersey and Pennsylvania. TOM TILL

Beams of sunlight cut through the fog in the Appalachian Mountains, New Jersey. TOM TILL

It is hard to remember that . . . everywhere we look the pavement has literally been laid down over a far older culture. On the Appalachian Trail . . . however, it is much easier to imagine that we are walking in Lenapehoking, the land of the Lenape.

—GLENN SCHERER & DON HOPEY,
Exploring the Appalachian Trail: Hikes in the Mid-Atlantic States

New growth protrudes from between quartzite rocks, New York. BART SMITH / CREST PHOTOGRAPHY

Daybreak, the Hudson River from Bear Mountain, New York

The Bear Mountain Bridge spans the Hudson River, New York.

I doubt if in the landscape there can be anything finer than a distant mountain range. They are a constant elevating influence.

—HENRY DAVID THOREAU, *Journal, 1858*

Elk Pen field is awash in fall hues, New York.

Mountain laurel blooms along a portion of the trail through Clarence Fahnstock State Park, New York.

The ruins of an abandoned church sit beside the trail near Dennytown Road, New York. BART SMITH / CREST PHOTOGRAPHY

The freezing spray from Kent Falls forms icicles on nearby rocks and trees, Connecticut. TOM TILL

A covered bridge overlooks the Housatonic River, Connecticut. TOM TILL

Bash Bish Falls State Park, Massachusetts LARRY ULRICH

MacKaye's original vision . . . was a utopian plan to develop the opportunities—for recreation, recuperation and employment.

—GUY & LAURA WATERMAN,
On the Trail's Founding Fathers

A hiker relaxes atop Mount Prospect, Massachusetts. A. BLAKE GARDNER

A New England town from "The Cobbles" overlook on a crisp October morning, Massachusetts BART SMITH

The mountain held the town as in a shadow.

—ROBERT FROST, "The Mountain"

Sunrise reflected on the Mill River, Vermont BART SMITH / CREST PHOTOGRAPHY

Mist rises over Little Rock Pond, Vermont. BART SMITH

October on Mosley Hill, Vermont BART SMITH / CREST PHOTOGRAPHY

A picturesque sunrise from inside Lookout Farm Cabin, Vermont BART SMITH / CREST PHOTOGRAPHY

Breathes there the man, with soul so dead,
Who never to himself has said,
This is my own, my native land!

—SIR WALTER SCOTT,
"The Lay of the Last Minstrel"

My, what big eyes you have! Gray tree frog, New Hampshire
ALAN BRIERE

They learn more in three days in the woods
than in three weeks in a classroom.

—RONALD M. FISHER, *The Appalachian Trail*

A hiker navigates the trail through the White Mountains, New Hampshire. LAURENCE PARENT

Great things are done when man and mountain meet;
This is not done by jostling in the street.

—WILLIAM BLAKE, *M.S. Notebooks*

The Presidential Range stretches to the horizon, White Mountain National Forest, New Hampshire.

Dawn's colors herald a new day over the White Mountains, New Hampshire.

Full many a glorious morning have I seen
Flatter the mountain-tops with sovereign eye,
Kissing with golden face the meadows green,
Gilding pale streams with heavenly alchemy.

—WILLIAM SHAKESPEARE,
"Sonnet 33"

Maples and birches create a vibrant fall landscape,
New Hampshire. TOM TILL

Lichen-encrusted boulders line Mount Washington near the timberline, New Hampshire. GEORGE WUERTHNER

Lake of the Clouds, White Mountain National Forest, New Hampshire BART SMITH

The golden foliage of an autumn birch, Crawford Notch State Park, New Hampshire GEORGE WUERTHNER

Dawn rises over the Mahoosuc Range, Maine.

A misty path cuts between Saddleback Mountain and
The Horn, Maine.

The Appalachian Trail offers many opportunities for solitude and reflection, Maine. *THIS PAGE*, BART SMITH / CREST PHOTOGRAPHY;
OPPOSITE, RICHARD V. PROCOPIO

White-tailed deer, Nesowadnehunk Stream, Maine RICHARD V. PROCOPIO

At three thousand feet . . . you come out into the open and, in the clean, cool air faintly spiced by the woods, find yourself in the domain of an assembly of great hills under pelts of forests and with rounded peaks lost in ruminations attuned to infinities of time.

—CHARLTON OGBURN, *The Continent in Our Hands*

Vibrant red leaves form a striking still life, Maine. RICHARD V. PROCOPIO

Tree and boulder become one, Maine. RICHARD V. PROCOPIO

Little Niagara Falls, Baxter State Park, Maine RICHARD V. PROCOPIO

A rainbow bursts forth from the storm clouds over Daicey Pond on Mount Katahdin, Maine. RICHARD V. PROCOPIO (THIS PAGE AND OPPOSITE)

There is a phenomenon called Trail Magic, known and spoken
of with reverence . . . which holds that often when things look
darkest some little piece of serendipity comes along to put you
back on a heavenly plane.

—BILL BRYSON, *A Walk in the Woods*

A moose on the loose ambles through Baxter State Park, Maine. TOM TILL

The vibrant colors of pine and mixed hardwood forests below Doubletop Mountain, Maine
TERRY DONNELLY

The whole point for the walkers who seek to follow the entirety of this beaten path is not getting to the top of the hill. It's going up there and not coming down again—not, at least, until they have found what they have lost, what they've gone looking for.

—ROBERT ALDEN RUBIN,
On the Beaten Path: An Appalachian Pilgrimage

A peaceful evening on Daicey Pond, Maine RICHARD V. PROCOPIO

Mount Katahdin as seen from Sentinel Mountain, Maine BART SMITH

So we would close the circle: As we had begun our adventure by climbing a mountain in Georgia, we would end it by descending one in Maine.

—RONALD M. FISHER, *The Appalachian Trail*

The Appalachian Trail . . . a footpath for those who seek fellowship with the wilderness.

—MICHAEL FROME, *The Evolution of Trails*

THEY MADE IT POSSIBLE

Appalachian Trail on My Mind would have been impossible to produce without the creative and technical skills of the professional photographers who succeeded in a difficult task—capturing the many moods and faces of the Appalachian Trail, from Georgia to Maine.

From the Great Smoky Mountains to the Berkshires, the Appalachian Trail contains a breathtaking array of beautiful images, but transforming these images into film requires more than just a camera. It takes an eye for composition, technical expertise, long hours of work, and the sheer determination to obtain a memorable shot rather than a mere snapshot.

The photographers who contributed to *Appalachian Trail on My Mind* provided this extra skill and effort. They hiked, climbed, waited, and watched to get the best possible images from all parts of the Trail.

To all the excellent photographers who contributed to *Appalachian Trail on my Mind,* thank you.

—THE GLOBE PEQUOT PRESS

Photographers in *Appalachian Trail on My Mind*
Mary Liz Austin
Alan Briere
Terry Donnelly
A. Blake Gardner
Laurence Parent
Richard V. Procopio
James Randklev
Bart Smith
Tom Till
Larry Ulrich
George Wuerthner
And these photo agencies:
Crest Photography
Tom Till Photography, Inc.
Larry Ulrich Stock Photography, Inc.
George Wuerthner Photography

SOURCE ACKNOWLEDGMENTS

The publisher gratefully acknowledges the following sources:

7, from *Georgia—78 Miles,* quoted in *The Appalachian Trail Reader,* ed. David Emblidge. Copyright 1996; Oxford University Press, Oxford.

9, 90, from *On the Beaten Path: An Appalachian Pilgrimage,* by Robert Alden Rubin. Copyright 2000; The Lyons Press, Guilford, Connecticut.

11, 63, quoted in *The Columbia World of Quotations.* Copyright 1996; Columbia University Press, New York.

13, from *Walking North,* quoted in *The Appalachian Trail Reader,* ed. David Emblidge. Copyright 1996; Oxford University Press, Oxford.

19, from *A Special Dignity in Naming,* quoted in *The Appalachian Trail Reader,* ed. David Emblidge. Copyright 1996; Oxford University Press, Oxford.

21, 37, quoted in *The Appalachian Trail,* by Ronald M. Fisher. Copyright 1972; National Geographic Society, Washington, D.C.

27, from *The Legend of Sleepy Hollow,* quoted in *Exploring America's Valleys.* Copyright 1984; National Geographic Society, Washington, D.C.

28, from "Song of the Open Road," quoted in *The Appalachian Trail Reader,* ed. David Emblidge. Copyright 1996; Oxford University Press, Oxford.

33, from *The Appalachian Trail Reader,* ed. David Emblidge. Copyright 1996; Oxford University Press, Oxford.

45, 87, from *A Walk in the Woods,* by Bill Bryson. Copyright 1998; Broadway Books, New York.

49, from *The Joan Baez Songbook.* Copyright 1972; Ryerson Music Publishers, New York.

51, from *Exploring the Appalachian Trail: Hikes in the Mid-Atlantic States,* by Glenn Scherer and Don Hopey. Copyright 1998; Stackpole Books, Mechanicsburg, Pennsylvania.

61, from *On the Trail's Founding Fathers,* quoted in *The Appalachian Trail Reader,* ed. David Emblidge. Copyright 1996; Oxford University Press, Oxford.

67, 70, 73, quoted in *The Concise Oxford Dictionary of Quotations.* Copyright 1981; Oxford University Press, New York.

68, 93, from *The Appalachian Trail,* by Ronald M. Fisher. Copyright 1972; National Geographic Society, Washington, D.C.

82, from *The Continent in Our Hands,* by Charlton Ogburn. Copyright 1971; William Morrow & Company, New York.

95, from *The Evolution of Trails,* quoted in *The Appalachian Trail Reader,* ed. David Emblidge. Copyright 1996; Oxford University Press, Oxford.